Songs of the Seder

A Music Book to Accompany the Passover Haggadah

Compiled, Edited, and Arranged by

Judith S. Rubenstein
and
Howard S. Rubenstein

GRANITE HILLS PRESS   •   EL CAJON

Songs of the Seder

Compiled and arranged by Judith S. Rubenstein and Howard S. Rubenstein
Translations and transliterations edited by Howard S. Rubenstein and Judith S. Rubenstein
Typography of music and lyrics by Judith S. Rubenstein

First Printing 1994
Second Printing 1995

Published by
GRANITE HILLS PRESS™
2175 Euclid Avenue
El Cajon, CA 92019-2664

SAN 298-072X

Printed on recycled paper with soy-based inks and aqueous materials

Cataloging in Publication Data

Songs of the Seder : a music book to accompany the Passover Haggadah /
   compiled, edited, and arranged by Judith S. Rubenstein and Howard
   S. Rubenstein.
      p. cm.
      English and Hebrew.
      Includes bibliographical references and indexes.
      ISBN 0-9638886-1-7
      1. Passover music. 2. Haggadot--Songs and music. 3. Seder--
Liturgy--Songs and music. 4. Judaism--Liturgy--Songs and music.
5. Haggadah.   I. Rubenstein, Judith S. II. Rubenstein, Howard S.

M2017.6.S65 1993   782.29'176'015241
                             QBI93-22462

Printed in the United States of America

CONTENTS

ACKNOWLEDGMENTS

We are indebted to many people and sources in the compilation of *Songs of the Seder*. Almost all the songs in this book are part of the great Jewish heritage of Passover music that has been passed down from generation to generation. We learned most of these songs as children, and some as adults. All the songs we knew we taught to our children, and we had the joy of having our children teach us the delightful "Beer-ckhaht Hah-mah-zone" melody they learned at camp. When we were not clear on details of melody or lyrics, we consulted the works listed in our Sources, and we are deeply grateful for this scholarship. Three sources were particularly valuable: Ellen M. Eggar's *A Singing Haggadah*, Paul Zim's *The Paul Zim Passover Seder* (recording), and Harry Coopersmith's *The Songs We Sing*. In *Songs of the Seder*, we made our own arrangements and transpositions to keys that we found pleasant and easy to sing and play.

We are grateful that Mr. and Mrs. Harry Coopersmith were Howard's music teachers at Anshe Emet Synagogue in Chicago when he attended Sunday School there. The Coopersmiths left Howard with a memory of joy in Jewish music and of excellence in music teaching. Howard learned "To the Red Sea" firsthand from the Coopersmiths, and he has never forgotten it.

We thank our editor, Rebecca Rauff, for her many helpful suggestions particularly in regard to notation. We thank Lynn Edington-Hogg, Director of the Music Department Record Library and Computer Laboratory at San Diego State University, for introducing Judith to the technique of computerized musical notation. We thank Miss Lorina Havill of South Orange, New Jersey, graduate of the Julliard School of Music, who was Judith's piano teacher in the 1950s.

We are indebted to our parents, Kalman and Martha Selig and Sidney and Selma Rubenstein, for the Jewish education, both formal and informal, that they provided us. The memory of Kalman's beautiful renditions of songs at Passover has been particularly influential upon us.

We wish to thank our children for participating enthusiastically in our Seders and for offering insightful advice and criticism. They helped in very specific ways in the formation of this music book: Emily years ago entered portions of the first version of our haggadah, *Becoming Free,* on her computer and showed us that it could be done; John made us computer literate by lending us his computer and teaching us how to use it; Adam helped us select and install our own computer that gave us independence and the capabilities necessary for transcribing music; and Jennifer tested and played on her guitar all the arrangements of songs in this collection and edited them with many useful suggestions particularly in regard to key and chords.

Although we cannot adequately thank all the people for their help in the creation of this book, we take sole responsibility for any errors it may contain.

INTRODUCTION

Purpose

The purpose of *Songs of the Seder* is to combine the music and lyrics of Passover songs in one compact volume that can accompany any haggadah. We have found a need for such a book. Most haggadahs do not contain music, and many people do not know the melodies of the Passover songs or the relationship between the rhythm of the music and the syllables of the words. The excellent collections of Jewish music listed in our Sources either include more Passover songs than families tend to sing or are large anthologies covering liturgy and festivals in addition to Passover. Their very size and comprehensiveness, so valuable to teachers and scholars, make them impractical for Seder use. *Songs of the Seder* is a conveniently sized paperback book. It presents essential songs in the order in which they appear in the Seder and with arrangements that are easy to sing and play.

Content

Songs of the Seder contains twenty-three songs, prayers, and chants that we have selected and adapted from a vast pool mostly of traditional Ashkenazi and contemporary Israeli (Sephardic) melodies. The line between song, prayer, and chant is sometimes difficult to draw. Therefore, in this book, all three types of melodies are loosely referred to as "songs" since all are set to transcribed music. The word "traditional," when used in this book to identify the source of a song, means "traditional Ashkenazi."

In this collection are sixteen Hebrew songs and one Aramaic song, "Ckhahd Gahd-yah," which are presented in transliteration. Four of these songs are also presented in English translation as songs in their own right with their own English titles, for example, "An Only Kid." The remaining two songs are American: one, "To the Red Sea," was written for Passover; the other, "Go Down, Moses," is an African-American slave spiritual which simply and eloquently expresses the feelings of Hebrew slavery.

With a single exception, we have included only one version of each song, that which we consider the most beautiful or that which is being taught most frequently today. In the case of "Mah Neesh-tah-nah," we present both the Israeli (Sephardic) and the traditional (Ashkenazi) melodies: the Israeli is currently widely taught, but the Ashkenazi is such a fundamental part of Jewish history and is so concise and pure that we could not bring ourselves to discard it.

Format

The musical arrangements are as simple as possible while maintaining the character of each song. To that end we have endeavored to do the following:
1. transcribe the melodies in clear, large notes;
2. use only the treble staff;
3. use only single notes for the melody;

4. use the four simplest keys: C major and its relative minor key A minor (with no sharps or flats), and G major and its relative minor key E minor (with only one sharp);

5. indicate guitar and piano chords above the melody, and provide a chart on the back cover for easy reference to decode the chords. On the chart, we have indicated the key signature relationship between the major and relative minor keys, and we have presented the three basic chords in each key. Usually, you will need only three chords to accompany any one song. You will need a total of only ten chords to accompany all the songs in this book (two of the chords appear in two keys, so the total number of chords is ten, not twelve). Although instrumental accompaniment is not currently common or even necessary at the Seder table, a guitarist or other musician among the guests who wishes to accompany the songs certainly adds to the pleasure of the festivities;

6. pitch the songs in a middle voice range for ease of singing for the greatest number of singers. (Probably not coincidentally this range is the same as the four simplest keys);

7. provide transliterations of all Hebrew songs. Our transliteration system follows English phonetics with one necessary modification: for the gutteral sound that does not exist in English, we use the letters **ckh** as in *bah-roockh*;

8. provide meaningful and non-derogatory edited translations of verses. In keeping with the overall spirit of the Seder typified by the "Essar Mah-kote" (the Ten Plagues and the Diminishing of Joy), we do not gloat over the disasters of our enemies. Thus, in our treatment of "It Would Have Been Enough" (the English version of "Dah-yay-noo"), we have eliminated verses that are in conflict with the spirit and intent of the rest of the Seder;

9. adapt and shorten some of the songs, particularly those which we have observed people start to sing, only to abandon in defeat because the songs turned out to be too long and complicated to complete;

10. treat English versions of the songs like songs in their own right. They are given English titles, for example, "It Would Have Been Enough," and the lyrics are transcribed under the notes to aid in singing;

11. show clearly the attachment of a note to a particular word or syllable for both English and transliterated versions in order to eliminate the guesswork in multi-syllabic phrases.

We expect that the content of *Songs of the Seder*, presented in a simple and accessible format, will greatly enhance the pleasure of your Seder.

To the Red Sea

Words by S. S. Grossman
Music by S. E. Goldfarb
Arranged by Judith S. and Howard S. Rubenstein

This song is fun to sing while marching to the Seder table.

Hee-nay Mah Tove

(Behold How Good)

Psalm 133:1
Folk Song
Arranged by Judith S. Rubenstein

Slowly and tenderly
Sing in unison* or as a round**

Part 1

Hee- nay mah tove oo- mah nah- yeem

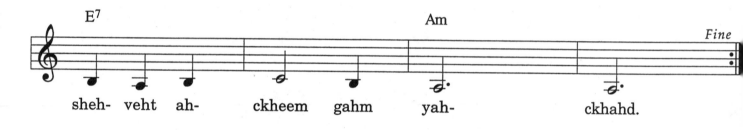

sheh- veht ah- ckheem gahm yah- ckhahd. *Fine*

Part 2

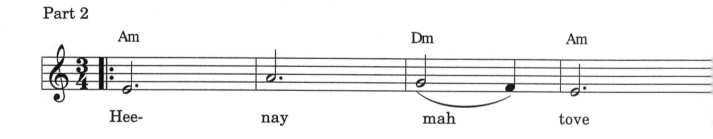

Hee- nay mah tove

sheh- veht ah- ckheem gahm yah- ckhahd. *2nd time D.C. al Fine*

Behold how good and pleasant it is for brothers and sisters to dwell together in unity!

Seated at the table, hold hands and sway rhythmically while singing.
*Sing Part 1 twice, then Part 2 twice, repeat as often as desired, and end with Part 1.
**Group A sings Part 1 twice; when Group A begins Part 2, then Group B begins Part 1.

L'-hahd-leek Nehr
(Thanksgiving for Light)

Traditional
Arranged by Judith S. and Howard S. Rubenstein

Slowly, with awe

Bah- roockh ah- tah Ah- doe- nye, eh- loh- hay- noo meh- leckh

hah- oh- lahm, ah- sher keed- shah- noo b'- meetz-

voe- tahv, v'- tzee- vah- noo

l'- hahd- leek nehr l'- hahd- leek nehr shel
*shel Shab- bat v'-

yome tove.
shel yome tove.

We give thanks to you, O God, our God, ruler of the universe, who gives us light.
In commemoration of this wondrous act, we light candles on the Sabbath and all our festivals.

* When the festival (yome tove) falls on Shabbat, sing this line instead of the words immediately above it.

Boe-ray P'-ree Hah-gah-fen

(Thanksgiving for the Fruit of the Vine)

Reverently, with free rhythm
allowing expression

Traditional
Arranged by Judith S. and Howard S. Rubenstein

Bah- roockh ah- tah Ah- doe- nye, eh- loh-

hay- noo meh- leckh hah- oh- lahm, boe-

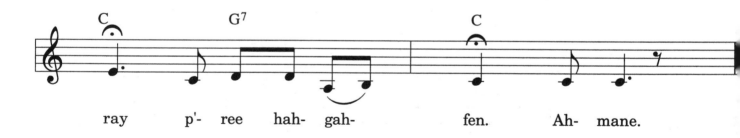

ray p'- ree hah- gah- fen. Ah- mane.

(Continue directly to the "Bah-ckhar Bah-noo")

We give thanks to you, O God, our God, ruler of the universe, who creates the fruit of the vine.

Bah-ckhar Bah-noo

(Thanksgiving for Passover and Other Festivals)

Traditional
Arranged by Judith S. and Howard S. Rubenstein

We give thanks to you, O God, our God, ruler of the universe,
who has chosen us from all nations for your service by blessing us with your commandments.

You have given us Holy Days, seasons of joy, and the festival of Passover.
We join to remember our last night of slavery and our Exodus from Egypt.
We give thanks to you, O God, our God, who blesses Israel and her festivals.

vah- noo vah- ckhar- tah, v'-oh- tah- noo kee- dahsh- tah mee-

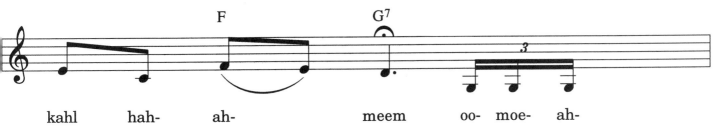

kahl hah- ah- meem oo- moe- ah-

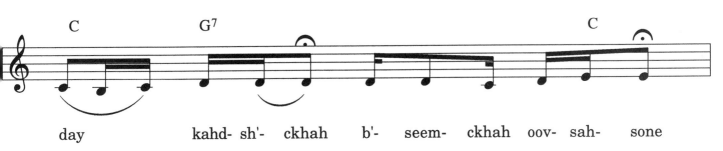

day kahd- sh'- ckhah b'- seem- ckhah oov- sah- sone

Slowly, with emphasis

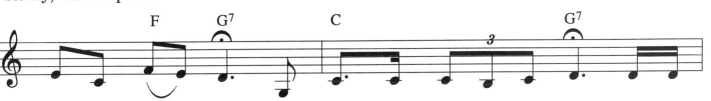

heen- ckhal tah- noo: Bah- roockh ah- tah Ah- doe- nye, m'- kah-

daysh yees- rah- ale v'- hahz- mah- neem:

(Continue directly to the "Sh'-heh-ckheh-yah-noo")

Sh'-heh-ckheh-yah-noo
(Thanksgiving for Life)

Reverently, with joy

Traditional
Arranged by Judith S. and Howard S. Rubenstein

We give thanks to you, O God, our God, ruler of the universe,
who has given us life, sustained us, and enabled us to reach this season.

Mah Neesh-tah-nah?

(The Four Questions)

Rhythmically
and with spirit

Traditional words, Israeli melody
Arranged by Judith S. Rubenstein

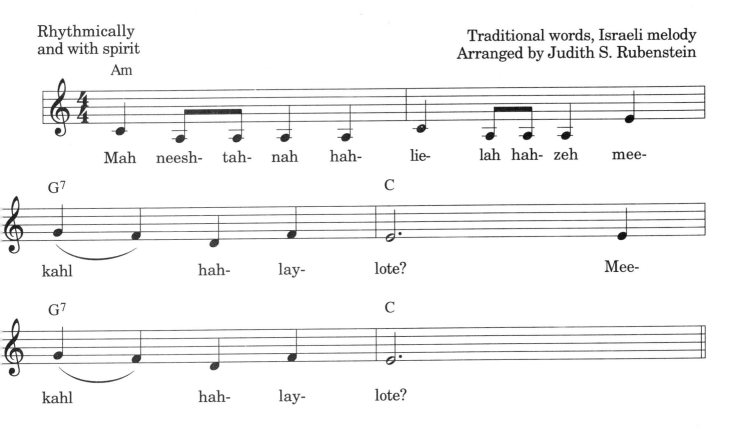

Why is this night different from all other nights?

Question 1: On all other nights we may eat either leavened or unleavened bread.
Why on this night must we eat only matzah, unleavened bread?

Question 2: On all other nights we may eat any kind of herbs.
Why on this night must we eat bitter herbs?

Question 3: On all other nights we do not have to dip vegetables even once.
Why on this night must we dip them twice?

Question 4: On all other nights we may eat either sitting up or reclining.
Why on this night must we recline?*

*We suggest that this fourth question is inappropriate and should be replaced with "Why on this night must we all sit erect or even stand?" This concept is explained in our haggadah *Becoming Free.*

(Repeat for each of the four questions)

1-4. Sheh- b'- ckhahl hah- lay- lote
1. ah- noo ohckh- leen ckhah-
2. ah- noo ohckh- leen sh'-
3. ayn ah-noo maht- bee- leen ah-
4. ah- noo ohckh- leen bain yoesh-

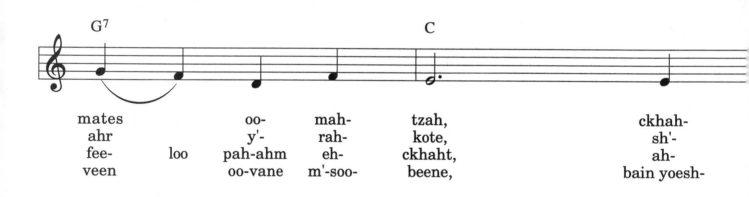

mates　　oo-　mah-　tzah,　　ckhah-
ahr　　y'-　rah-　kote,　　sh'-
fee-　loo　pah-ahm　eh-　ckhaht,　　ah-
veen　　oo-vane　m'-soo-　beene,　　bain yoesh-

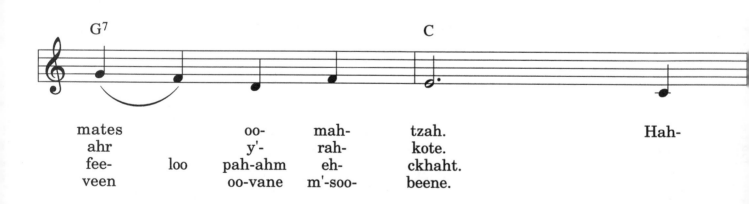

mates　　oo-　mah-　tzah.
ahr　　y'-　rah-　kote.
fee-　loo　pah-ahm　eh-　ckhaht.
veen　　oo-vane　m'-soo-　beene.　　Hah-

10

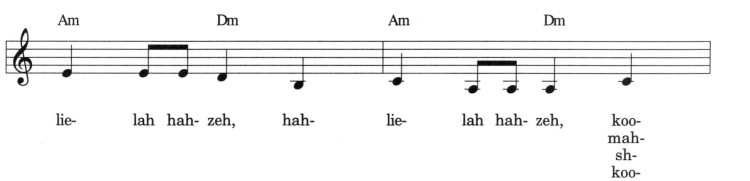

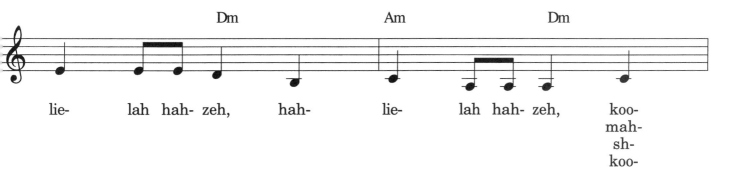

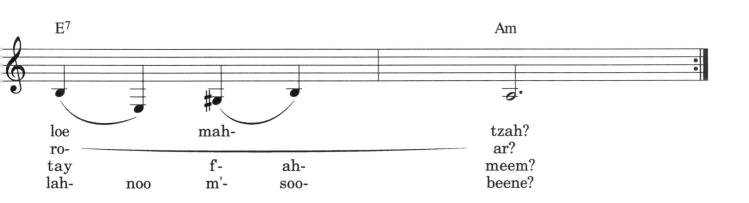

Mah Neesh-tah-nah?
(The Four Questions)

Traditional
Arranged by Judith S. and Howard S. Rubenstein

Chant rhythmically
but freely

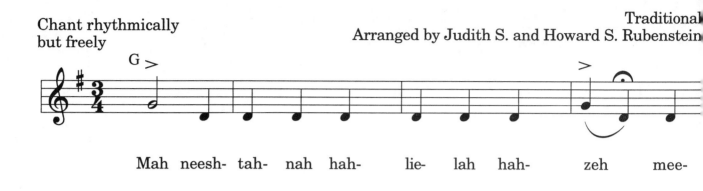

Mah neesh- tah- nah hah- lie- lah hah- zeh mee-

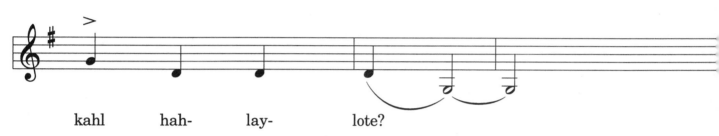

kahl hah- lay- lote?

Why is this night different from all other nights?

Question 1: On all other nights we may eat either leavened or unleavened bread.
Why on this night must we eat only matzah, unleavened bread?

Question 2: On all other nights we may eat any kind of herbs.
Why on this night must we eat bitter herbs?

Question 3: On all other nights we do not have to dip vegetables even once.
Why on this night must we dip them twice?

Question 4: On all other nights we may eat either sitting up or reclining.
Why on this night must we recline?*

*We suggest that this fourth question is inappropriate and should be replaced with "Why on this night must we all sit erect or even stand?" This concept is explained in our haggadah *Becoming Free*.

(Repeat for each of the four questions)

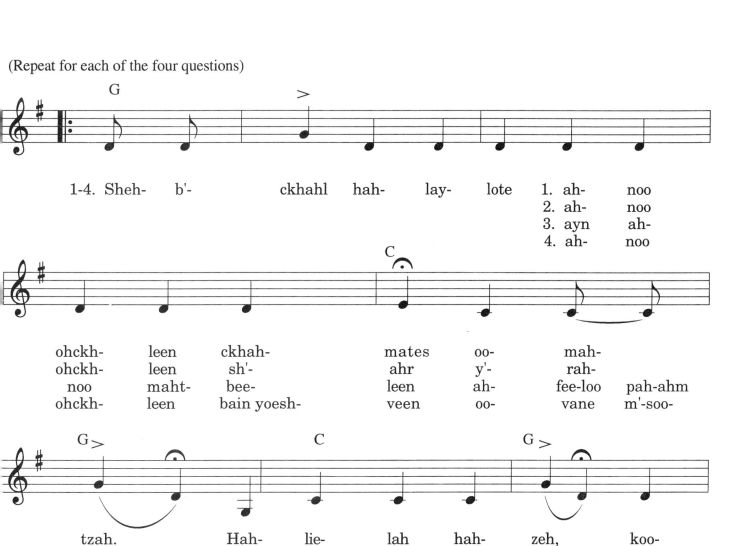

1-4. Sheh-	b'-	ckhahl hah-	lay-	lote	1. ah- noo
					2. ah- noo
					3. ayn ah-
					4. ah- noo

ohckh-   leen   ckhah-   mates   oo-   mah-
ohckh-   leen   sh'-   ahr   y'-   rah-
noo   maht-   bee-   leen   ah-   fee-loo   pah-ahm
ohckh-   leen   bain yoesh-   veen   oo-   vane   m'-soo-

tzah.   Hah-   lie-   lah   hah-   zeh,   koo-
kote.   mah-
eh-   ckhaht.   sh'-
beene.   koo-

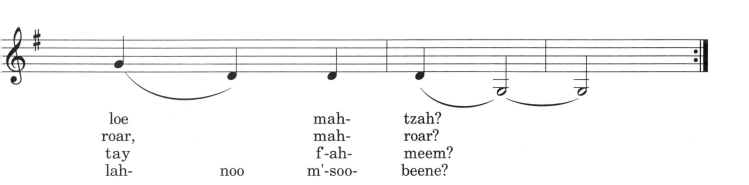

loe   mah-   tzah?
roar,   mah-   roar?
tay   f'-ah- meem?
lah-   noo   m'-soo- beene?

Go Down, Moses

African-American slave spiritual
Arranged by Judith S. Rubenstein

Slowly, with deep feeling

1. When Is- rael was in E- gypt land,
2. Thus saith the Lord, in bold Mo- ses said,
3. As Is- rael stood by the wa- ter side,

Let my peo- ple go. Op- pressed so hard they
If not, I'll smite your
By God's com- mand it

could not stand, Let my peo- ple go.
first- born dead,
did di- vide,

Chorus

Go down, Mo- ses, way down in

E- gypt land. Tell old Pha- raoh to

let my peo- ple go.

14

Dahm
(The Ten Plagues)

Slowly, rhythmically,
like tolling bells

Traditional
Arranged by Judith S. Rubenstein

"Dahm" is a dirge-like chant. The transliteration is sung. The English is spoken. "Dahm" can be sung responsively, with the leader chanting the Hebrew and the group saying the English.

Dah-yay-noo

(It Would Have Been Enough)

Traditional
Arranged by Judith S. and Howard S. Rubenstein

God performed many miracles for the Hebrews, any one of which "would have been enough."
The next song, "It Would Have Been Enough," freely translates "Dah-yay-noo" of which Verse 1
and the Chorus are transliterated here.

It Would Have Been Enough
(Dah-yay-noo)

Rapidly and in high spirits

Traditional
Arranged by Judith S. and Howard S. Rubenstein

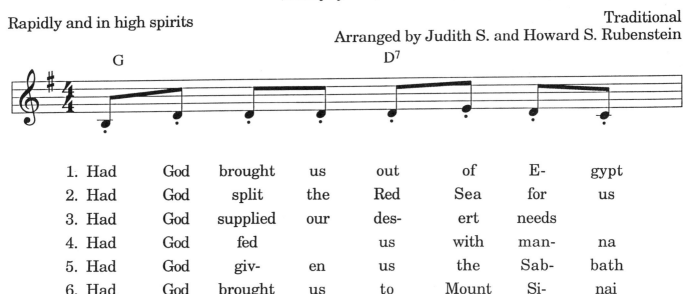

1. Had God brought us out of E- gypt
2. Had God split the Red Sea for us
3. Had God supplied our des- ert needs
4. Had God fed us with man- na
5. Had God giv- en us the Sab- bath
6. Had God brought us to Mount Si- nai
7. Had God giv- en us the To- rah

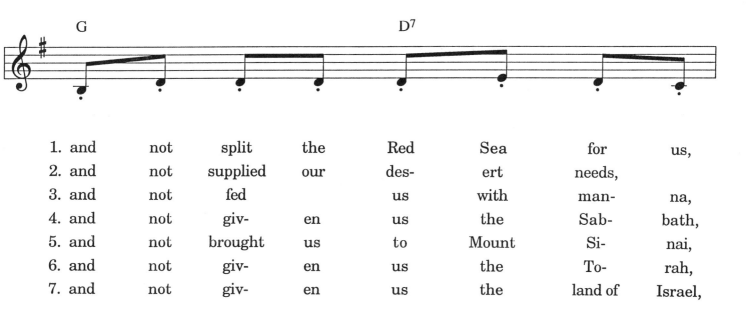

1. and not split the Red Sea for us,
2. and not supplied our des- ert needs,
3. and not fed us with man- na,
4. and not giv- en us the Sab- bath,
5. and not brought us to Mount Si- nai,
6. and not giv- en us the To- rah,
7. and not giv- en us the land of Israel,

God performed many miracles in freeing the Hebrews from slavery in Egypt, any one of which "would have been enough." This song describes some of the miracles and paraphrases "Dah-yay-noo."

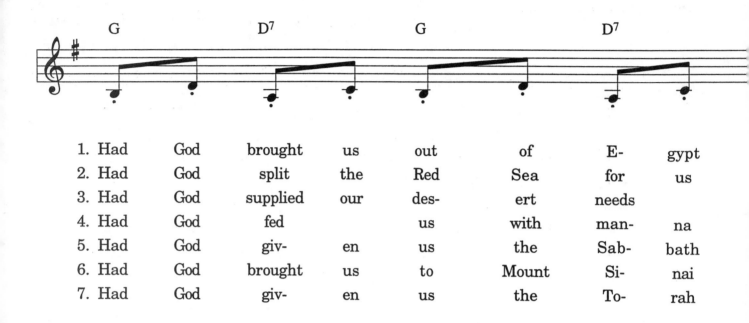

1. Had	God	brought	us	out	of	E-	gypt
2. Had	God	split	the	Red	Sea	for	us
3. Had	God	supplied	our	des-	ert	needs	
4. Had	God	fed		us	with	man-	na
5. Had	God	giv-	en	us	the	Sab-	bath
6. Had	God	brought	us	to	Mount	Si-	nai
7. Had	God	giv-	en	us	the	To-	rah

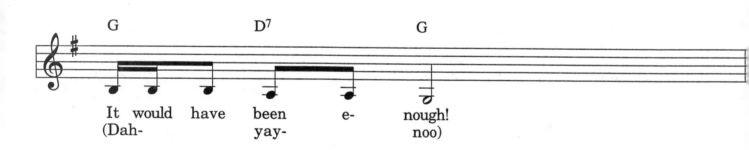

It would have been e- nough!
(Dah- yay- noo)

Chorus

Moe-tzee
(Thanksgiving for Bread)

Traditiona
Arranged by Judith S. and Howard S. Rubenstei

Reverently

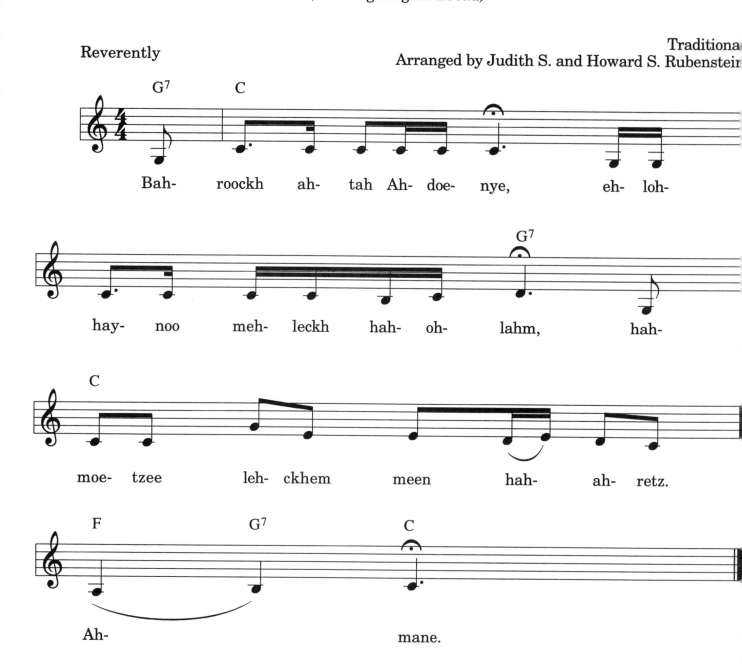

We give thanks to you, O God, our God, ruler of the universe,
Who brings forth from the earth grain for bread.

Beer-ckhaht Hah-mah-zone
(Grace after the Meal)

Traditional
Arranged by Judith S. and Howard S. Rubenstein

Joyfully, with reverence

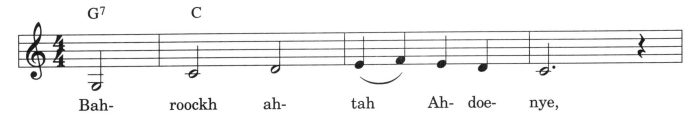

Bah- roockh ah- tah Ah- doe- nye,

eh- loh- hay- noo meh- leckh hah- oh- lahm,

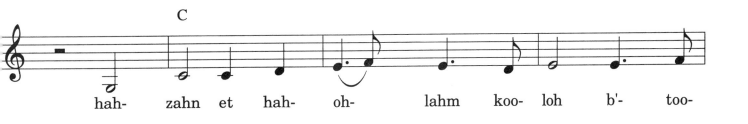

hah- zahn et hah- oh- lahm koo- loh b'- too-

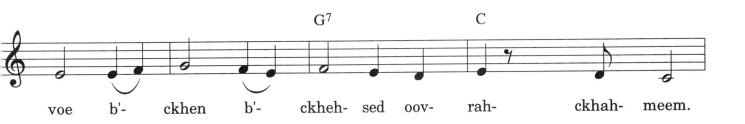

voe b'- ckhen b'- ckheh- sed oov- rah- ckhah- meem.

We give thanks to you, O God, our God, ruler of the universe,
whose food we have eaten and who has granted us the gift of life.

21

Hoo noe- ten leh- ckhem l'- ckhahl bah- sahr,

kee l'- oe- lahm ckhahss- doe, oov- too-

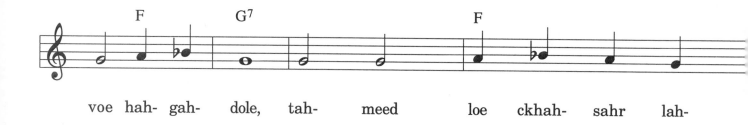

voe hah- gah- dole, tah- meed loe ckhah- sahr lah-

noo, v'- ahl yehckh- sahr lah- noo mah- zone l'- oh-

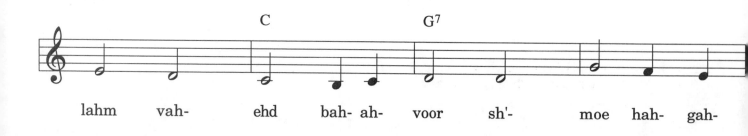

lahm vah- ehd bah- ah- voor sh'- moe hah- gah-

dole;　　　kee　hoo　el　zahn　oom-　fahr-　nayss　lah-

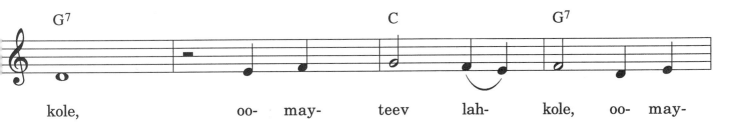

kole,　　　oo-　may-　teev　lah-　kole,　oo-　may-

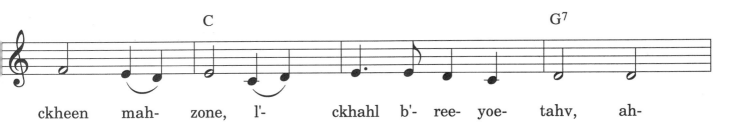

ckheen　mah-　zone,　l'-　ckhahl　b'-　ree-　yoe-　tahv,　ah-

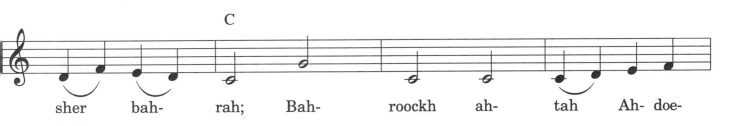

sher　bah-　rah;　Bah-　roockh　ah-　tah　Ah-　doe-

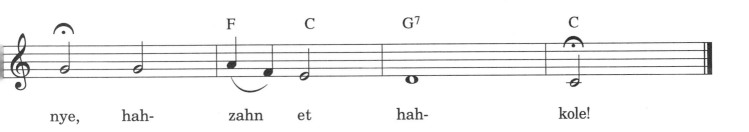

nye,　hah-　zahn　et　hah-　kole!

Ay-lee-yah-hoo Hah-nah-vee
(Elijah the Prophet)

Traditional
Arranged by Judith S. Rubenstein

May Elijah the prophet come even in our time with the Messiah, son of David.

Hallelujah!

(Sing How Splendid is God!)

Traditional
Arranged by Judith S. and Howard S. Rubenstein

With awe and joy

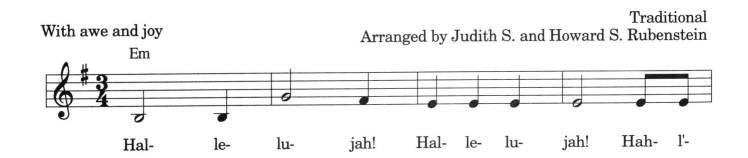

Hal- le- lu- jah! Hal- le- lu- jah! Hah- l'-

loo ahv- day Ah- doe- nye.

Hal- le- lu- jah! Hal- le- lu- jah! Hah- l'-

loo et shem Ah- doe- nye.

Sing how splendid is God!

Lah-shah-nah Hah-bah-ah!

(Next Year in Jerusalem!)

Traditional words, Israeli melody
Arranged by Judith S. and Howard S. Rubenstein

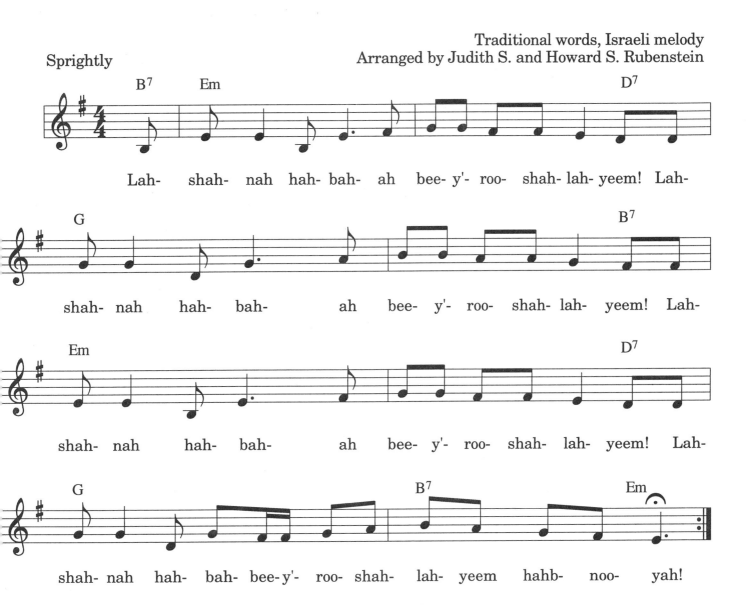

Next year in Jerusalem! Next year in a secure Jerusalem!

Ah-deer Hoo

(God of Might)

Traditional
Arranged by Judith S. and Howard S. Rubenstein

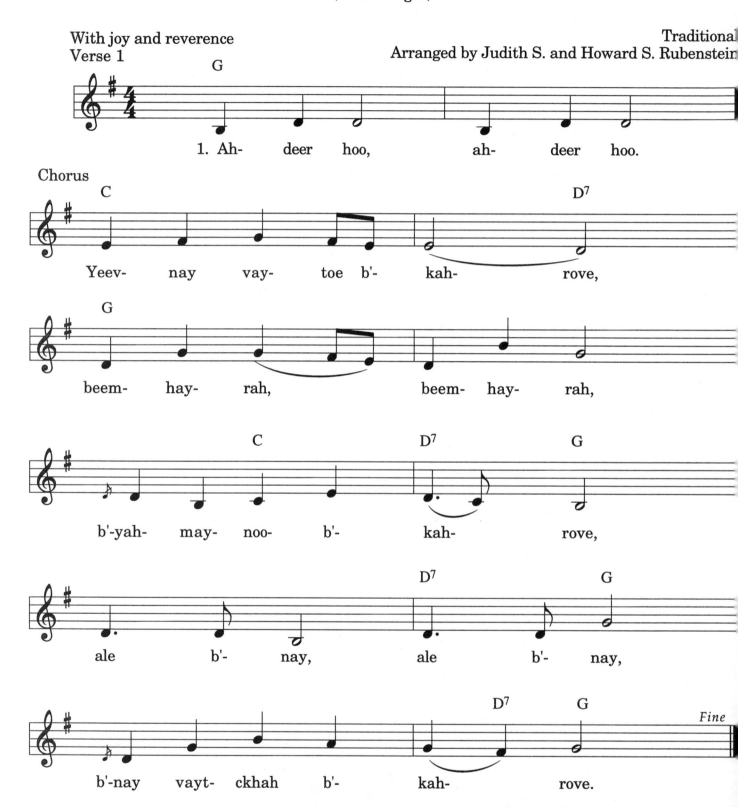

"Ah-deer Hoo" is a prayer for the restoration of the temple. "God of Might," which follows, freely paraphrases this song.

Verse 2

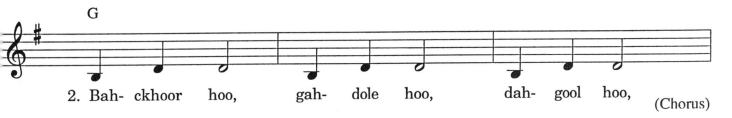

2. Bah- ckhoor hoo, gah- dole hoo, dah- gool hoo, (Chorus)

Verses 3-8   (Sing two verses at a time, then the Chorus)

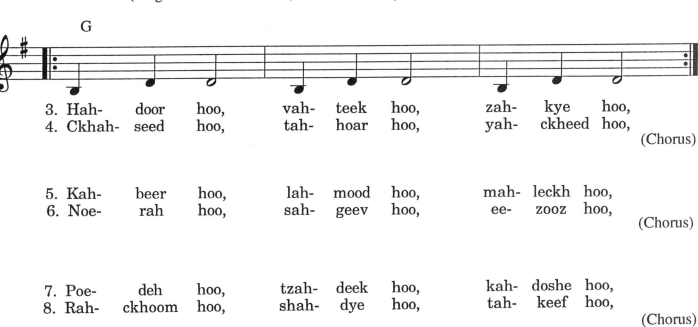

3. Hah- door hoo, vah- teek hoo, zah- kye hoo,
4. Ckhah- seed hoo, tah- hoar hoo, yah- ckheed hoo, (Chorus)

5. Kah- beer hoo, lah- mood hoo, mah- leckh hoo,
6. Noe- rah hoo, sah- geev hoo, ee- zooz hoo, (Chorus)

7. Poe- deh hoo, tzah- deek hoo, kah- doshe hoo,
8. Rah- ckhoom hoo, shah- dye hoo, tah- keef hoo, (Chorus)

God of Might
(Ah-deer Hoo)

With joy and reverence

Traditional
Arranged by Judith S. and Howard S. Rubenstein

1. God of Might, God of Right,
2. Then God gave to each slave

Thee we give all glo- a- ry.
pro- mised lib- er- tion.

Thine all praise in these days,
His great word Pha- raoh heard,

as in a- ges hoa- ry.
mak- ing a proc- la- ma- tion,

When we hear, year by year,
"Set them free to serve me

free- dom's won- drous sto- ry:
as a ho- ly na- tion."

"God of Might" is the traditional English rendition of "Ah-deer Hoo."

Eh-ckhahd Mee Yoe-day-ah?

(Who Knows One?)

Traditional words, Israeli melody
Arranged by Judith S. and Howard S. Rubenstein

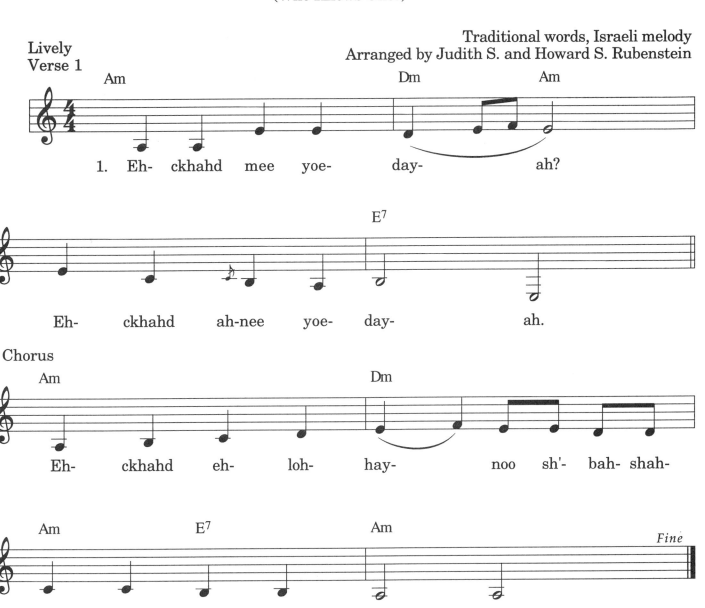

Lively
Verse 1

1. Eh- ckhahd mee yoe- day- ah?

Eh- ckhahd ah-nee yoe- day- ah.

Chorus

Eh- ckhahd eh- loh- hay- noo sh'- bah- shah-

mah- yeem oo- vah- ah- retz!

Fine

This song is cumulative and speeds up as it goes. This transliterated version presents verses 1, 2, and 13.
Verse 13 contains the key words of all 13 verses. The next song, "Who Knows One?," is the translation of
all 13 verses.

Who knows one? I know one. (Chorus): One God Almighty of heaven and earth.
Who knows two? I know two. Two stones of law . . . Three patriarchs . . .
Four matriarchs . . . Five books of Torah . . . Six parts of the Mishnah . . .
Seven days of the week . . . Eight days to circumcision . . . Nine months to childbirth . . .
Ten commandments . . . Eleven stars in Joseph's dream . . . Twelve tribes of Israel . . .
Thirteen attributes of God.

Verse 2

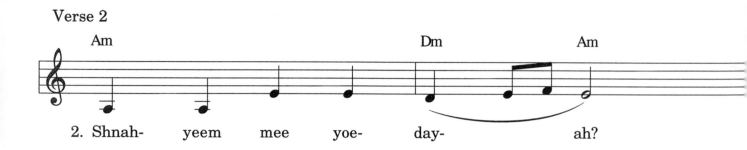

2. Shnah- yeem mee yoe- day- ah?

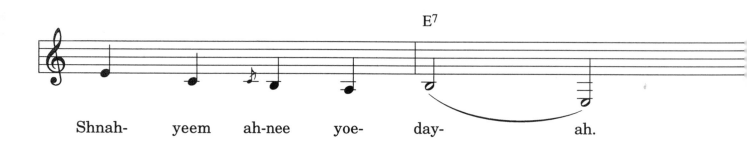

Shnah- yeem ah-nee yoe- day- ah.

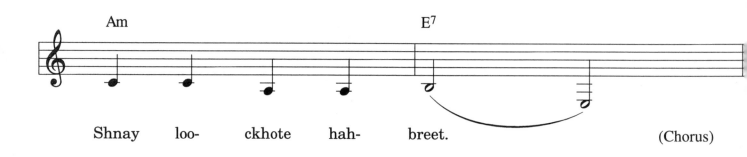

Shnay loo- ckhote hah- breet. (Chorus)

Verse 13   (Verse 13 includes all the previous [and omitted] verses and speeds up as it goes.)

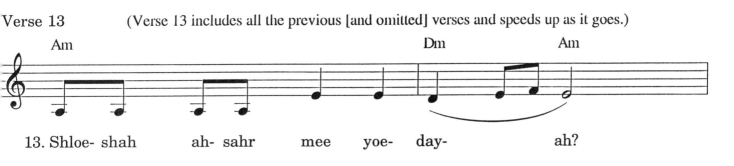

13. Shloe- shah   ah- sahr   mee   yoe- day-   ah?

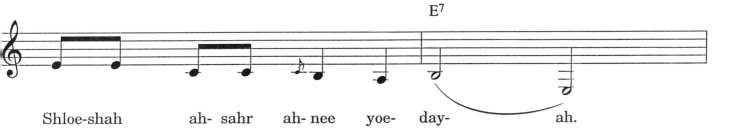

Shloe-shah   ah- sahr   ah- nee   yoe- day-   ah.

(Repeat music for all lines beneath and end with a rousing Chorus)

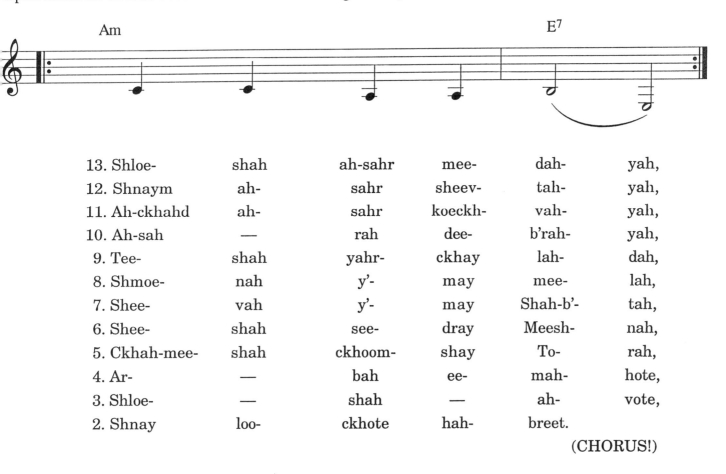

13. Shloe-	shah	ah-sahr	mee-	dah-	yah,
12. Shnaym	ah-	sahr	sheev-	tah-	yah,
11. Ah-ckhahd	ah-	sahr	koeckh-	vah-	yah,
10. Ah-sah	—	rah	dee-	b'rah-	yah,
9. Tee-	shah	yahr-	ckhay	lah-	dah,
8. Shmoe-	nah	y'-	may	mee-	lah,
7. Shee-	vah	y'-	may	Shah-b'-	tah,
6. Shee-	shah	see-	dray	Meesh-	nah,
5. Ckhah-mee-	shah	ckhoom-	shay	To-	rah,
4. Ar-	—	bah	ee-	mah-	hote,
3. Shloe-	—	shah	—	ah-	vote,
2. Shnay	loo-	ckhote	hah-	breet.	

(CHORUS!)

33

Who Knows One?
(Eh-ckhahd Mee Yoe-day-ah?)

Traditional words, Israeli melody
Arranged by Judith S. and Howard S. Rubenstein

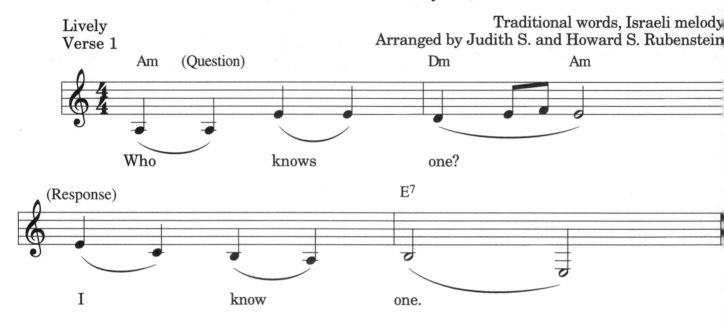

This song is cumulative and speeds up as it goes. Each verse repeats the ones before, beginning with the most recent, working backwards to the second, and ending with a rousing Chorus. This song is the translation of "Eh-ckhahd Mee Yoe-day-ah?"

The pattern of each verse is Question, Response, Answer. For example:
"Who knows one? I know one. One God Almighty of heaven and earth."
The song can be sung in two groups: Group A: Question, Group B: Response, A & B together: Answer.

Verse 6

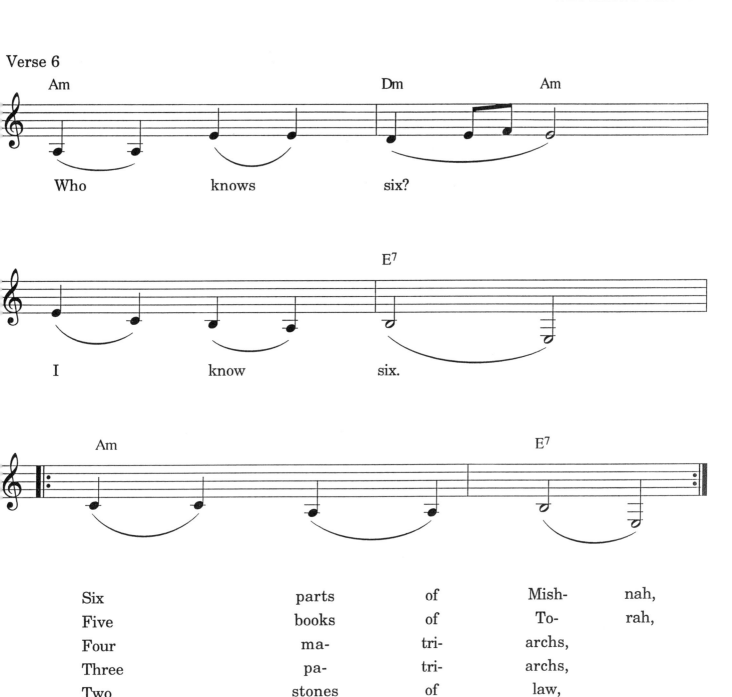

Who knows six?

I know six.

Six	parts	of	Mish-	nah,
Five	books	of	To-	rah,
Four	ma-	tri-	archs,	
Three	pa-	tri-	archs,	
Two	stones	of	law,	

(Chorus)

Verse 7

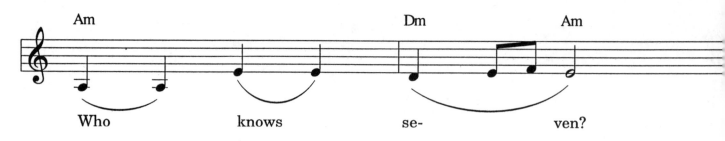

Who   knows   se-   ven?

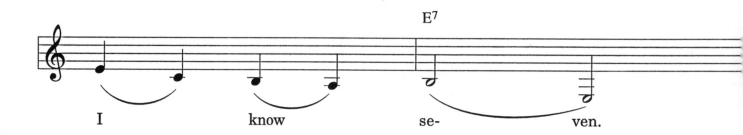

I   know   se-   ven.

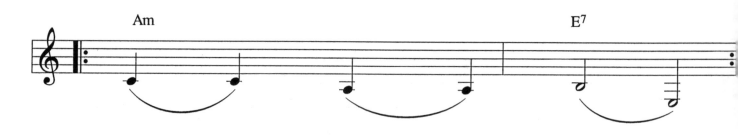

Sev-	en	days	of the	week,
Six		parts	of	Mish- nah,
Five		books	of	To- rah,
Four		ma-	tri-	archs,
Three		pa-	tri-	archs,
Two		stones	of	law,

(Chorus)

Verse 8

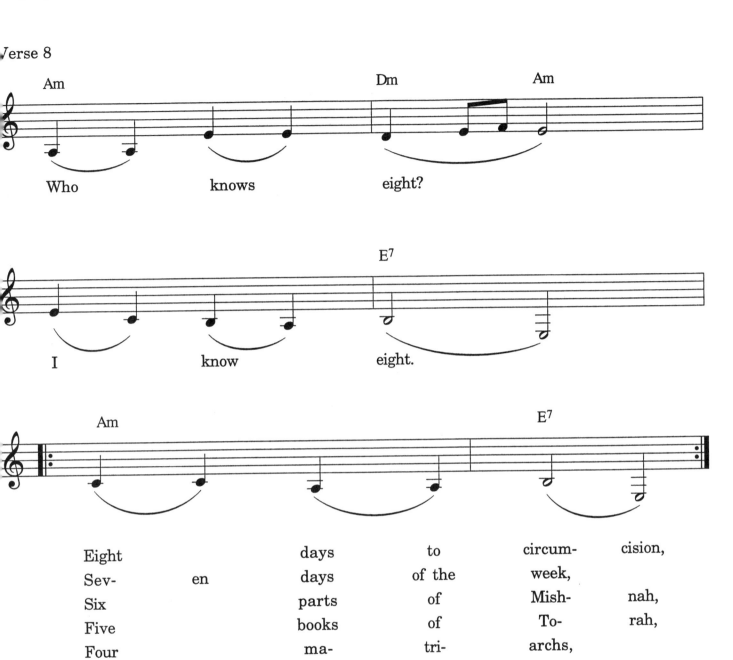

Eight		days	to	circum-	cision,
Sev-	en	days	of the	week,	
Six		parts	of	Mish-	nah,
Five		books	of	To-	rah,
Four		ma-	tri-	archs,	
Three		pa-	tri-	archs,	
Two		stones	of	law,	

(Chorus)

Verse 9

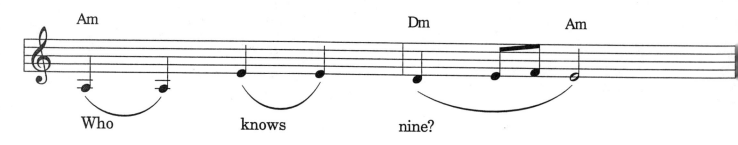

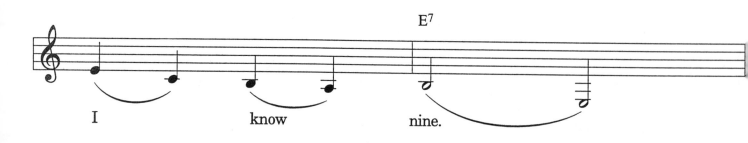

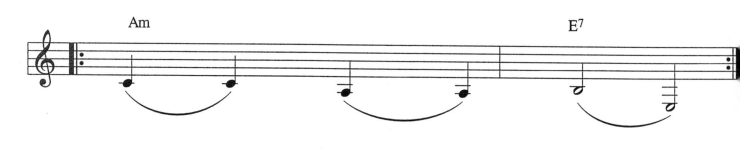

Nine		months	to	child-	birth,
Eight		days	to	circum-	cision,
Sev-	en	days	of the	week,	
Six		parts	of	Mish-	nah,
Five		books	of	To-	rah,
Four		ma-	tri-	archs,	
Three		pa-	tri-	archs,	
Two		stones	of	law,	

(Chorus)

Verse 10

Ten		Com-		mand-	ments,
Nine		months	to	child-	birth,
Eight		days	to	circum-	cision,
Sev-	en	days	of the	week,	
Six		parts	of	Mish-	nah,
Five		books	of	To-	rah,
Four		ma-	tri-	archs,	
Three		pa-	tri-	archs,	
Two		stones	of	law,	

(Chorus)

Verse 11

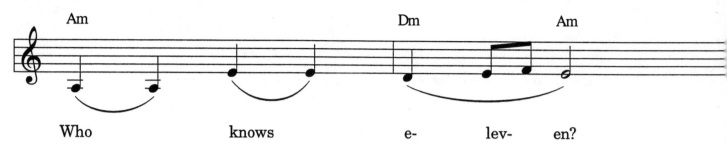

Who knows e- lev- en?

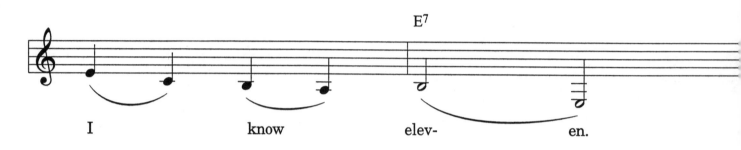

I know elev- en.

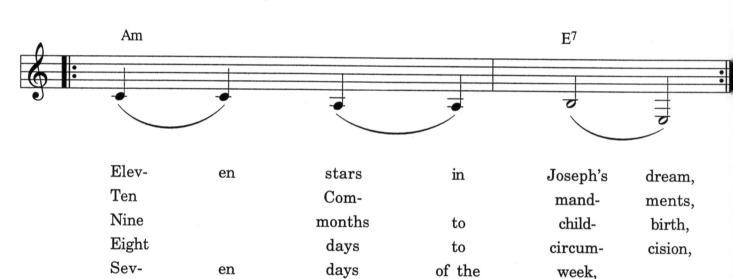

Elev-	en	stars	in	Joseph's	dream,
Ten		Com-		mand-	ments,
Nine		months	to	child-	birth,
Eight		days	to	circum-	cision,
Sev-	en	days	of the	week,	
Six		parts	of	Mish-	nah,
Five		books	of	To-	rah,
Four		ma-	tri-	archs,	
Three		pa-	tri-	archs,	
Two		stones	of	law,	

(Chorus)

Verse 12

Twelve		tribes	of	Isra-	el,
Elev-	en	stars	in	Joseph's	dream,
Ten		Com-		mand-	ments,
Nine		months	to	child-	birth,
Eight		days	to	circum-	cision,
Sev-	en	days	of the	week,	
Six		parts	of	Mish-	nah,
Five		books	of	To-	rah,
Four		ma-	tri-	archs,	
Three		pa-	tri-	archs,	
Two		stones	of	law,	

(Chorus)

Verse 13

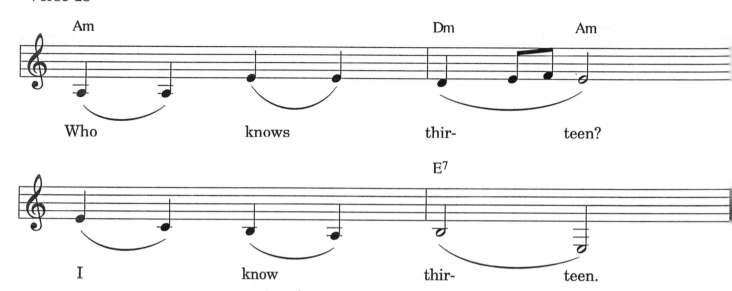

Who   knows   thir-   teen?

I   know   thir-   teen.

(Repeat music for all lines beneath and end with a rousing Chorus)

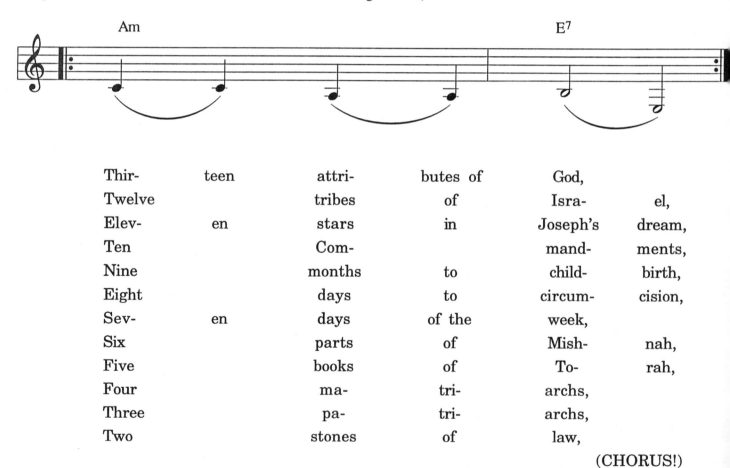

Thir-	teen	attri-	butes of	God,	
Twelve		tribes	of	Isra-	el,
Elev-	en	stars	in	Joseph's	dream,
Ten		Com-		mand-	ments,
Nine		months	to	child-	birth,
Eight		days	to	circum-	cision,
Sev-	en	days	of the	week,	
Six		parts	of	Mish-	nah,
Five		books	of	To-	rah,
Four		ma-	tri-	archs,	
Three		pa-	tri-	archs,	
Two		stones	of	law,	

(CHORUS!)

Ckhahd Gahd-yah

(An Only Kid)

Traditional
Arranged by Judith S. and Howard S. Rubenstein

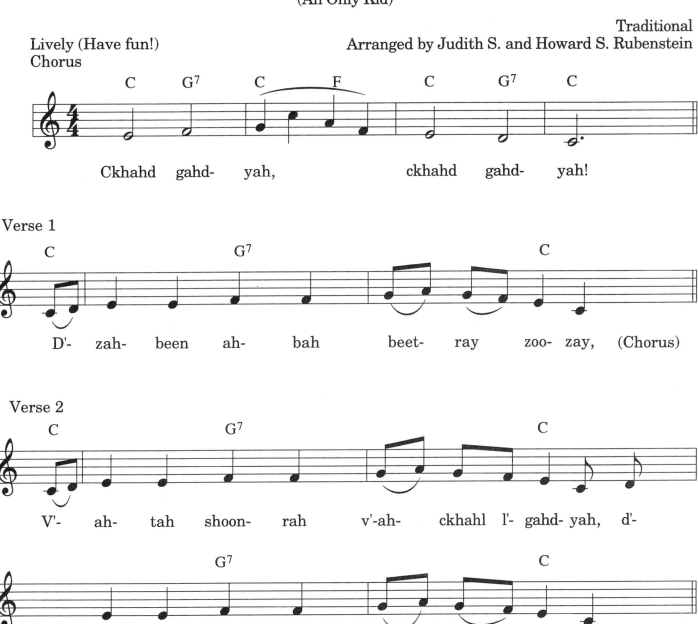

This song is in Aramaic and is cumulative. Verse 10 repeats all verses. Verses 1, 2, 3, 4, and 10 are transliterated here. The next song, "An Only Kid," (One Baby Goat) is the English translation of all 10 verses.

Verse 10: Then came the Almighty who destroyed the angel of death
that slew the butcher, that killed the ox, that drank the water, that quenched the fire,
that burned the stick, that beat the dog, that bit the cat, that ate the kid
my father bought for two zu-zeem. An only kid, an only kid!

An Only Kid

(Ckhahd Gahd-yah)

Lively (Have fun!)
Chorus

Traditional
Arranged by Judith S. and Howard S. Rubenstein

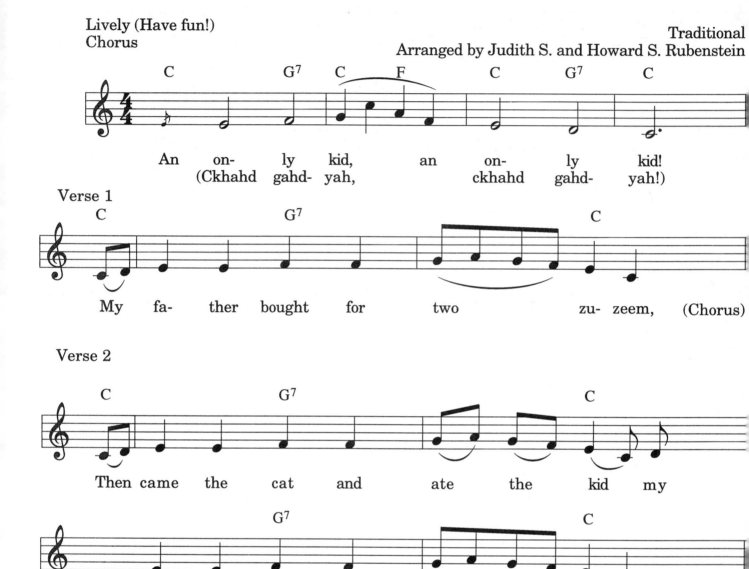

An on- ly kid, an on- ly kid!
(Ckhahd gahd- yah, an ckhahd gahd- yah!)

Verse 1

My fa- ther bought for two zu- zeem, (Chorus)

Verse 2

Then came the cat and ate the kid my

fa- ther bought for two zu- zeem, (Chorus)

"An Only Kid" is cumulative. Each verse repeats the ones before, beginning with the most recent, working backwards to the first, speeding up as it goes, and ending with a rousing Chorus.
This song translates the old Aramaic song "Ckhahd Gahd-yah" in which God destroys the angel of death. On this note of God's triumph, the Seder is concluded. Happy Passover!

Verse 5

Then came the fire and burned the stick, that

beat	the	dog,	that
bit	the	cat,	that
ate	the	kid	my

fa- ther bought for two zu- zeem, (Chorus)

Verse 6

Then came the water and quenched the fire, that

burned	the	stick,	that
beat	the	dog,	that
bit	the	cat,	that
ate	the	kid	my

fa- ther bought for two zu- zeem, (Chorus)

Verse 7

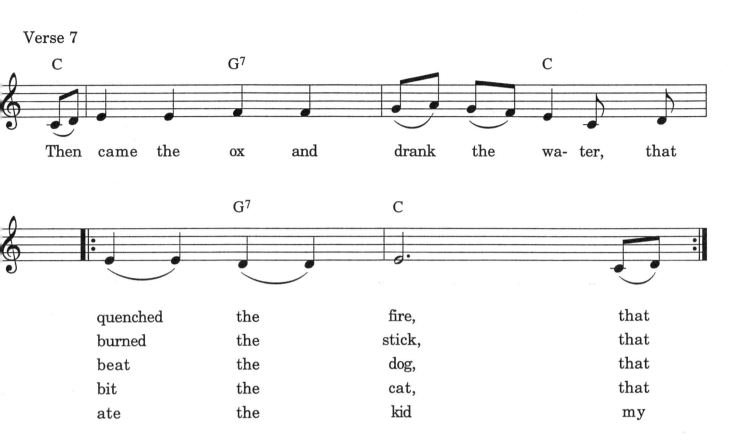

Then came the ox and drank the wa- ter, that

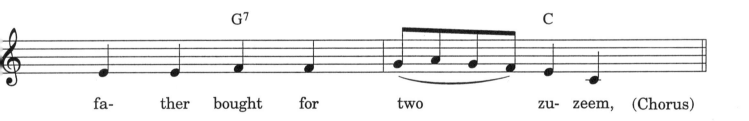

quenched	the	fire,	that
burned	the	stick,	that
beat	the	dog,	that
bit	the	cat,	that
ate	the	kid	my

fa- ther bought for two zu- zeem, (Chorus)

Verse 8

Then came the butcher and killed the ox, that

drank	the	water, that
quenched	the	fire, that
burned	the	stick, that
beat	the	dog, that
bit	the	cat, that
ate	the	kid my

fa- ther bought for two zu- zeem, (Chorus)

Verse 9

Then came the angel of death and slew the butch- er, that

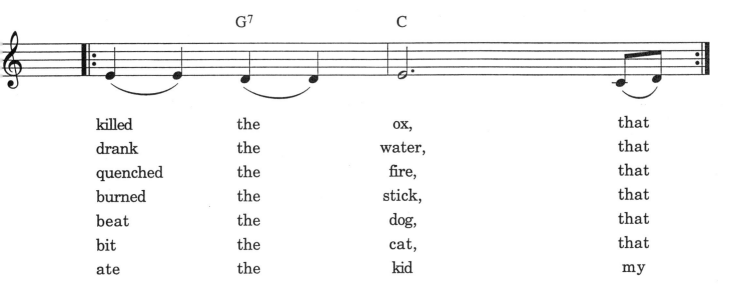

killed	the	ox,	that
drank	the	water,	that
quenched	the	fire,	that
burned	the	stick,	that
beat	the	dog,	that
bit	the	cat,	that
ate	the	kid	my

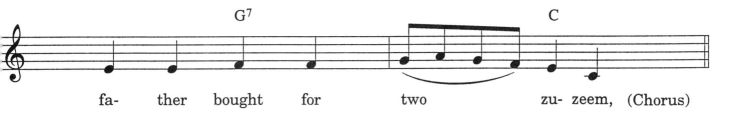

fa- ther bought for two zu- zeem, (Chorus)

SOURCES

Carp, Bernard, Ph.D., ed. *The Jewish Songster.* New York: National Jewish Welfare Board, 1949.

Coopersmith, Harry, ed. and comp. *The Songs We Sing.* New York: United Synagogue Commission on Jewish Education, 1950.

Egger, Ellen M., comp., trans., and illus. *A Singing Haggadah.* Princeton: L'Rakia Press, 410 Nassau Street, Princeton, NJ 08540, 1986.

Goldfarb, Israel, and Samuel E. Goldfarb, eds. *The Jewish Songster: Music for Voice and Piano,* Part I. Fourth Revised Edition. New York: Religious Schools of Congregation Beth Israel Anshe Emes, Harrison Street, Brooklyn, 1925.

Pasternak, Velvel, ed., comp., and arr. *Israel in Song.* New York: TARA Publications, 1974.

Rubenstein, Howard S., and Judith S. Rubenstein, eds. and comps. *Becoming Free: A Biblically Oriented Haggadah for Passover: The Permanent Relevance of the Ancient Lesson.* El Cajon: Granite Hills Press, 2175 Euclid Avenue, El Cajon, CA 92019-2664, 1993.

Zim, Paul. *The Paul Zim Passover Seder.* [Sound cassette #33091.] Box 310, Forest Hills, New York: Simcha Recordings, 1991.

INDEX OF TITLES

INDEX OF FIRST LINES

ABOUT THE EDITORS

JUDITH SELIG RUBENSTEIN was born in New York in 1942. She grew up in Maplewood, New Jersey, where she graduated from Columbia High School, was active in Reform Jewish youth groups, and was confirmed at Temple Israel (South Orange). She received her B.A. from Wellesley College, and M.A.T. and Doctorate in Education from Harvard University. She is a teacher of English as a Second Language and Adult Basic Education; the senior author of *Essentials of Reading and Writing English*, an adult literacy series published by National Textbook Company; and the author of numerous articles on topics including education, children's concepts as related to their religion, and explaining Hanukah to Christians. The emphasis of her writings has been to make specialized information available to the general public.

HOWARD S. RUBENSTEIN was born in Chicago in 1931. He received his Jewish education mostly at Anshe Emet Synagogue when Solomon Goldman was rabbi and Moses Silverman cantor. His principal mentors were Ben Aronin and Mr. and Mrs. Harry Coopersmith. He graduated from Lake View High School, Chicago, and received a B.A. degree *magna cum laude* from Carleton College, where he was elected to Phi Beta Kappa and Sigma Xi (the national college science honor society) and was awarded the Noyes Greek Prize. He received an M.D. from Harvard University and served his internship and residency in medicine at the Los Angeles County Hospital. He returned to Harvard Medical School to conduct research in the Departments of Surgery, Bacteriology and Immunology, and Pathology. He then joined the Harvard University Health Services, where he was physician and chief of allergy from 1966-1989. In 1989, Dr. Rubenstein "retired" to San Diego in order to write, raise fruit trees, and become a medical consultant to the Department of Social Services. In addition to medicine and agriculture, Judaism (in the first centuries of the Christian era) and early Christianity (prior to the deification of Jesus and the creation of the Trinity in the fourth century) have been major interests, and he has published articles on these subjects.

Howard and Judith married in 1968 and have four children, Emily, Adam, Jennifer, and John. In the mid-1980s, the Rubensteins were copresidents of the Winchester Jewish Community in Winchester, Massachusetts. Howard frequently led the holiday celebrations, including the community Seder (the "Second Seder") and the Rosh Hashanah and Hanukah parties. Judith, playing the guitar, led the singing. Judith was the first Jewish representative to the Winchester Ecumenical Society. *Songs of the Seder* is Howard and Judith's second book published together. The first was *Becoming Free: A Biblically Oriented Haggadah for Passover*. In 1994 the Rubensteins were elected to membership in the San Diego Writers & Editors Guild.